Thomas S. Owens

FOOTBALL STADIUMS

The Millbrook Press   Brookfield, Connecticut

To Diana Star Helmer

Designed by Thomas Morlock   Cover photograph courtesy of Corbis

Photographs courtesy of NFL Photos: pp. 1 (© Al Messerschmidt), 4, 9 (© Greg Crisp), 10 (© Bob Rosato), 11 (© Tony Tomsic), 18-19 (© Al Messerschmidt), 29 (© James V. Biever), 38, 54 (© James D. Smith); AP/Wide World Photos: pp. 5, 17, 24-25, 53; HOK Sport: p. 13; © SportsChrome USA/Rob Tringali Jr.: pp. 20, 48-49; The Ottawa Citizen: p. 34; Allsport: pp. 35 (© Jonathan Daniel), 42 (©Damian Strohmeyer), 46 (© Larry French); Warner Studio: p. 56; The National Football League: p. 60

Library of Congress Cataloging-in-Publication Data

Owens, Tom, 1960-

Football Stadiums/ by Thomas S. Owens

p. cm. — (Sports palaces)

Includes biographical references (p.) and index.

ISBN 0-7613-1764-3 (lib. bdg.)

1. Football stadiums — United States — History. 2. Football stadiums — United States — Finance.

I. Title.   II. Series.

GV415 .O94 2001

796.332′06′80973-dc21   00-020413

Published by The Millbrook Press, Inc.

2 Old New Milford Road

Brookfield, Connecticut 06804

www.millbrookpress.com

Printed in Hong Kong

1 3 5 4 2

Contents

Introduction   4

Chapter One   Building Dreams   6

Chapter Two   Big Feats Grow from Small Wonders   12

Chapter Three   Change Is Part of the Game   16

Chapter Four   Passing the Bucks   22

Chapter Five   Running with the Pack   28

Chapter Six   Surprising Stadiums   33

Chapter Seven   Where Work Is Play   37

Chapter Eight   More Than a Game   45

Chapter Nine   Can Future Stadiums Preserve the Past?   52

For Further Information   61

Index   62

Introduction

The loyalty fans feel toward their favorite football teams and players is legendary. Some fans get just as passionate about football stadiums. After all, a field is just a field without seating for the fans who come to watch.

Lawrence Lee Jr. is a New York Jets fan from Staten Island, New York, who feels deeply about stadiums. He saw the Jets play many games at Giants Stadium and elsewhere. But of all the games he saw his team play, it was the one he saw at Shea Stadium that he enjoyed most. Somehow Shea — a park built with baseball in mind — had "a feeling of home" that other stadiums didn't.

"First was the natural grass field," Lee said. "How much more of a 'home feeling' can you get? I can remember my first visit to Shea Stadium, in the early 1970s. . . . Never before had I seen such a large, uninterrupted plot of grass! And here, grown men got to play ball on it every day. One thing I have never forgotten is this: Every time I walked through the tunnel, and finally 'into' the stadium, I caught the smell of freshly cut grass. I know how it sounds, but it's true. That smell of grass I still get today."

Lee later realized something else special about Shea: "Like many ballparks, Shea is open-ended along what is [baseball's] outfield wall. Because of this, and even though Shea has a very large scoreboard, you can see the surrounding neighborhood. You can see the large globe that was built for the 1964 World's

THE NEW YORK JETS PLAY BOTH AT GIANTS STADIUM IN EAST RUTHERFORD, NJ, AND SHEA STADIUM IN FLUSHING MEADOW, NY. HERE, JETS FANS PACKED INTO SHEA STADIUM IN 1974 TO SEE QUARTERBACK JOE NAMATH LEAD THEIR TEAM TO A 17–14 VICTORY OVER MIAMI.

Fair. You can see other buildings, trees, and even airplanes from the nearby airport when they fly overhead. A real feeling of sitting outside, 'in the open,' as it were."

Part of a neighborhood. Part of the world. To Lee, that is what football is. "Football, at least to me, is meant to be played on a natural grass field, not a rug. To see players' uniforms all dirty by the end of the game showed how hard they actually worked to try and win the game. As kids, when we played football, we loved it when we got all dirty. It almost united us with the pros — we got just as dirty, and fought just as hard for the touchdowns we scored."

Football isn't just for Sunday afternoons. It's for Saturdays in backyards and sports pages any morning. Football is a part of life, like buildings, trees, airplanes, and dirt. For many fans, football is a part of home. That's why football's homes are so important.

1

BUILDING DREAMS

While National Football League teams come to Kansas City to play the Chiefs, NFL owners may come to the city to meet another famed name in the sport.

The HOK Sports Facilities Group uses the initials of three company founders (Hellmuth, Obata, and Kassabaum). This architectural company had designed new stadiums or helped design renovations for existing stadiums for all but two NFL teams going into the year 2000 — thirty of thirty-two.

The HOK Sports "team" started in the stadium design and redesign business in 1983. Fifteen years later its football statistics had grown to superstar status. Of the eight new stadiums that opened in the 1990s, HOK Sports created seven of them — the TWA Dome in St. Louis, Missouri; Raymond James Stadium in Tampa Bay, Florida; PSINet Stadium in Baltimore, Maryland; Browns Stadium in Cleveland, Ohio; FedEx Field in Washington, D.C.; Ericsson Stadium in Charlotte, North Carolina; and Adelphia Coliseum in Nashville, Tennessee.

How did this team work?

The Right Site

Dennis Wellner, HOK senior vice president, said that one job of serving a sports team is site selection. In other words, it's the "where" of stadium design.

"The basic test is size," he said. "Would the type of stadium a team wants fit on this site? We like new stadiums to be downtown. We don't want to be out in the country. We want to be where more people are. Downtowns and stadiums can help each other. However, land isn't always available. Sometimes, it has to be cleared [of old buildings]."

Next, can people park near the stadium? Or are there other ways to get there: bus, train, or boat?

"We look at traffic flow, to see if fans could get to the stadium and home easily," Wellner said. "Then, we see if a site could supply enough of the utilities — electricity, gas, water, and sewage — to support a stadium."

HOK helps teams decide how big or small to make their new stadiums. "If a team has the goal of hosting a Super Bowl, the stadium has to have a minimum of 70,000 seats," Wellner said. "For weekly games, capacity in the mid to low 60,000 range is okay."

Seeing the Big Picture

Because fans want to see the game as "up-close" as possible, scoreboards are vital parts of the stadiums.

"There are a limited number of companies that manufacture scoreboards of this size," Wellner said. That's why some scoreboards made in the late 1980s were still being used ten years later. Older scoreboards often measured 24 by 36 feet (7 by 11 m) and used a cathode-ray tube, the type of picture display found in older television sets.

But in places like Baltimore, Tampa Bay, and Cleveland, LED (light-emitting diode) screens came into use before the turn of the twenty-first century, Wellner said. Scoreboards used to keep the same proportions of

THE 49ERS' FIRST HOME, KEZAR STADIUM, AROSE IN 1922. IN GOLDEN GATE PARK, THE STADIUM WAS BUILT WHERE AN OLD PLANT NURSERY AND STABLE STOOD, AS WELL AS A RHODODENDRON GARDEN.

WHEN TEXAS STADIUM OPENED IN DALLAS IN 1971, DALLAS CITIZENS DEVISED A UNIQUE WAY TO USE THE SPACE WHEN THE COWBOYS DIDN'T NEED IT. THE HUGE PARKING LOTS WERE TRANSFORMED INTO A DRIVE-IN MOVIE THEATER! PEOPLE PAID TO WATCH HOLLYWOOD MOVIES WHILE SITTING IN THEIR PARKED CARS. THE THREE SCREENS WERE FOLDED DOWN ON GAME DAYS.

height to width as TV screens. "But in these three stadiums," Wellner said, "the screens are much wider."

A Field for Play

HOK not only gives teams a place to play in but also a classy field to play on.

"We have a group here called HOK Turf, which designs field systems," Wellner said. "We work with agronomists about grass types, which grasses will grow best in certain parts of the country, in different climates.

"All the outdoor stadiums we've done have all-natural grass. That's what teams want to play on," Wellner continued. "We make sure our design doesn't block out sun, keeping the grass from growing. Grass needs natural sunlight. Of HOK-created stadiums, only the TWA Dome in St. Louis has artificial turf. [But] systems are being toyed with that would grow grass outside during the week. The grass would be rolled in [on platforms] for the game."

Baltimore's natural-grass stadium debuted in 1998, with the aid of 90 HOK Sports architects and some 59,863 design hours.

A Good Fit

HOK Sports was the natural choice to create PSINet Stadium. The firm had designed Oriole Park at Camden Yards, and the two sports arenas were to share one 85-acre (34-hectare) stretch of land — a sports complex.

LED SCREENS LIKE THIS ONE IN TAMPA BAY'S STADIUM MAY REACH 27 FEET (8 M) HIGH AND STRETCH 97 FEET (30 M) ACROSS.

"Typically, stadium designers do not take their inspiration from ballparks. But we could not ignore the tremendous impact Oriole Park has on this sports complex," said Ron Labinski, HOK Sports project adviser. The HOK team worked to make sure that "the football stadium fits gracefully into the context of its historic neighborhood." HOK held meetings with neighborhood residents, collecting their concerns about lighting, noise, and traffic before finalizing a design.

Breaking with tradition, HOK divided the upper deck of the Baltimore Ravens field into four different sections. Each segment looks like the letter "V." Team publicity calls the upper deck's design "victory notches."

THE VICTORY NOTCHES AT CAMDEN YARDS ALLOW FANS TO SEE GLIMPSES OF THE BALTIMORE SKYLINE—AND PEOPLE PASSING BY THE STADIUM CAN PEEK AT THE GAME'S ACTION.

Chilling Out in Cleveland

In Cleveland, HOK was challenged by Mother Nature. Designers remembered how the Browns' past home near Lake Erie was nicknamed "Mistake on the Lake." Legend had it that winds would swirl in cyclone like patterns, freezing fans. To keep things slightly warmer at the new stadium — but without adding a grass-killing roof — HOK Sports decided that wind screens might do the trick. Out of the sight lines of fans along the concourse and upper deck, HOK would place 4- by 8-foot (1.2- by 2.4-m) aluminum panels pierced with 3/4-inch (1.9-centimeter) holes that would reduce incoming winds by up to 75 percent.

Cleveland's cityscape added challenges, too. The city government ruled against new light towers, because the height could cross the flight path of the nearby airport. HOK didn't want columns in the stadium blocking the sight lines of fans. So the designers developed an overhang around the stadium rim, tilted up from the fans to allow as much natural light as possible. For night games, the overhang was rimmed with lights.

Room to Grow

HOK's first work in the NFL was planning Miami's Joe Robbie (now Pro Player) Stadium. That facility opened in 1987. But how long will this — or any of the stadiums — last?

"Stadiums don't have a limited physical life expectancy. If they're maintained, they could last 100 years," Wellner said. "The reason newer stadiums are being torn down is because they can't provide amenities for fans. There are not enough toilets or concession stands. Fans need stairs and ramps. Provisions should be made for persons with disabilities. A person in a wheelchair should be able to sit anywhere in the stadium."

Wellner pointed out that meeting the needs of fans should be balanced by meeting the business needs of team owners. "Team owners need club-level seats and suites to [rent, to] help pay the incredible salaries of players. That's the business of football." And that's why, Wellner said, "You build areas of the stadium that can expand. . . ."

AT NIGHT, THE LIGHTS THAT RIM CLEVELAND'S STADIUM GIVE IT THE APPEARANCE OF A GLOWING HALO.

2

BIG FEATS GROW FROM SMALL WONDERS

At HOK Sports Facilities Group, Peter Friederich is a "model" employee. His job title is Chief Modelmaker and Shop Manager.

"I grew up on the New Jersey shore, near a river," Friederich said. "I must have been eight years old when I made my first model of a ship. I wanted to be an architect. I went to architecture school at New York University. In school, you have to build lots of models."

Next Friederich worked for an architectural firm. After building a model for a client in 1984, he decided to "try to make a living at it." Models are more than a job for Friederich. "I still like building ship models," he said from his office. "I'll be awake sometimes until three o'clock in the morning working on my own models. It's fun and relaxing. And I get to keep them. Unfortunately, you don't get to keep the stadium models we make."

His co-workers share his passion. At HOK, Friederich works with a crew of seven — four men and three women. By 1999, three members of the group had been together for six years. "Not to brag," he said, "but this [department] is the best part of the whole place! We have a laser to cut tiny pieces. For materials, we use everything — Plexiglas, styrene, different hardwoods, glass, steel. We'll try any material, if it seems durable."

"Durable" may be an understatement. "Our models typically weigh anywhere from 80 to 300 pounds (36 to 136 kg). That's because of all the plastics we use. Plastics get heavy when piled on top of each other," Friederich said. "Even so, when we ship models, we custom crate them [in] specially designed boxes for shipping." Despite the weight, "the models are fragile, and we want them protected. They are like any other one-of-a-kind works of art."

MODELS LIKE THIS ONE OF TAMPA BAY'S STADIUM CAN WEIGH HUNDREDS OF POUNDS, YET THEY ARE FRAGILE AND MUST BE MOVED WITH CARE.

Shrinking Stadiums

Most HOK models are built in one of three scales: 1:16, where 1 inch on the model equals 16 feet on the actual building; 1:32 (1 inch equals 32 feet); or 1:100 (1 inch equals 100 feet). For a 1:32 scale, the model might be a square 45 inches to a side.

"The smallest we ever built," Friederich said, "was a section model, 2 inches by 1 inch. For a 'Bring Your Kids to Work' day, we had eighty kids here in the office. We put together a model kit for each of them to assemble. They each built a section of Cleveland's Jacobs Field."

Teams often get the pleasure of "touring" models. "They will show the public what they are getting," Friederich said. This can help convince the government to give money for stadium construction. "The model is a marketing tool. It helps sell season tickets, if fans can be shown just where they'll be sitting. They can imagine their sight line. An owner may [even] want a model to keep for himself."

In building a model, Friederich wants to do more than just show a stadium. "We want to get the surrounding city right and accurate, down to the color of the grass. We do a lot of work on the Internet, to make sure we know what roads and existing buildings look like." Sometimes, Friederich will even bring a study model out to a site. And, of course, "I'll take a lot of pictures."

"It's called 'scratch' building," Friederich explained. "Everything is by scratch. We start with 4- by 8-foot [1.2- by 2.4-m] sheets of Plexiglas. We'll do castings [make molds] for a small model part like a seat. Then we can reproduce thousands of those seats. We get tiny pieces of lead [for] people and cars. Then we shape and paint them. We'll sculpt the trees. For a recent stadium, our landscape department planned on placing cypress trees outside the stadium. We went to the public library to check out tree books, to see pictures of those trees. We're at the library all the time for research."

Toying with Ideas

Is a chief modelmaker's job anything like assembling a model kit bought in a toy department? "Absolutely!" says Friederich, "You have a set of instructions from the box. You have to clean the parts, sand them, glue them, and paint them in sequence. My instructions are a set of architectural blueprints. I build the site, then work on each level of a stadium, going up. The big difference is that in a model kit, all the parts are there!"

By the start of the twenty-first century, Friederich had been building for fifteen years. "When I first started, CAD [computer-aided design] was becoming popular. I thought then computers could replace models." But even though HOK has a computer department dedicated to 3-D graphics and animations for stadiums, Friederich said, "My work has tripled in the last three years. You can't replace a model you can touch with your hands. You can get down, see through the windows, and look on the field. You can't get that with a computer."

For example, he said, "For the new Steelers stadium, we made several section models. Often, we'll make three highly detailed models. We may make ten models of different areas. Smaller models serve as a study and design tool. To work out an idea in three-dimensional form, it's easier for a client to [envision the finished project with] a model than a 3-D drawing."

Models may be better than computer drawings, but nothing beats the real thing — even to a modelmaker. "To go to a stadium after it's built, and to know that you built the same thing in miniature — it's great!" Friederich said. What Friederich builds day by day will someday become something huge and grand, a home for athletes and their fans. But for Friederich, day by day, it's simpler. "You're building neat stuff: Toys!"

MEETING THE PUBLIC IS A TREAT FOR MANY MODELMAKERS, WHO TEND TO SPEND A LOT OF TIME BEHIND THE SCENES. "WHEN WE OPENED RAVENS STADIUM," MODELBUILDER FRIEDERICH SAID, "I WAS WALKING AROUND THE HARBOR AREA IN BALTIMORE. I SAW A CROWD OF PEOPLE STANDING AROUND. THEY WERE LOOKING AT ONE OF MY MODELS." FRIEDERICH COULDN'T RESIST WANDERING OVER TO DISCUSS THE MODEL, TOO. WHEN ONE OF THE WOMEN COMMENTED THAT HE SEEMED TO KNOW A LOT ABOUT THE SUBJECT, FRIEDERICH REVEALED HIS IDENTITY. "THAT WAS FUN!"

3

CHANGE IS PART OF THE GAME

Football evolved throughout the twentieth century, and so did the construction of football stadiums.

As the twentieth century closed, the oldest surviving NFL stadium was Chicago's Soldier Field. It was built to honor American soldiers of World War I, and construction began in 1919.

Soldier Field was originally designed to hold 100,000 fans. During a 1954 religious service, 260,000 people packed into the park. Today's fans might look around and wonder how Soldier Field ever held so many fans. The answer: The field used to be bigger. Today's bleachers are built across one end of the field. Nearly one-third of the original stadium is unused, except for parking by employees. Soldier Field was downsized to make it more suitable for football — fans want to be part of the game.

Other teams took note. When Cleveland rejoined the NFL in 1999, it kept the Browns name but built a new stadium "with the goal in mind to keep the fans as close to the action as possible," said team vice president Alex Martins.

"One of the ways you accomplish that is a steep pitch," Martins said, calling the slope found in the new stadium "a little steeper than what fans are accustomed to from Cleveland Municipal, but it's not dangerous."

CHICAGO'S SOLDIER FIELD RESTS ON 10,000 PILE FOUNDATIONS DRIVEN AN AVERAGE DEPTH OF 62.5 FEET (19 M) INTO LANDFILL ADDED TO WHAT WAS ONCE A PART OF LAKE MICHIGAN. THE STADIUM IS RINGED BY TWO ROWS OF 32 STONE COLUMNS, GIVING IT THE APPEARANCE OF AN ANCIENT ROMAN PLAYING FIELD.

Fan Comfort

Today's teams also factor the comfort of fans into their building plans.

Cleveland allowed a roomy width of 21 inches (53 cm) for club seats, 19 to 21 inches (48 to 53 cm) for lower-priced general seats. And before the stadium opened, Browns president Carmen Policy spent four hours in July getting a fan's-eye view of the new stadium to judge which seats would be the best and worst. Although one section was sold as "obstructed" because one end zone was not fully viewable, most fans considered Cleveland sight lines an improvement over the many obstructed views in other stadiums.

ONE OF THE LAST CHANGES EVER MADE TO CLEVELAND MUNICIPAL STADIUM (USED THROUGH 1995) WAS LOWERING THE FIELD BY 2 FEET (61 CM). WHY? FRONT-ROW FANS COULDN'T SEE OVER PHOTOGRAPHERS, REFEREES, AND OTHER SIDELINES PEOPLE BLOCKING THE VIEW OF THE ACTION.

THE GRASS USED IN THE TITANS' STADIUM WAS "TIFSPORT BERMUDA" AND HAD GROWN FOR A YEAR BEFORE BEING REPLANTED ON THE FIELD. EACH SOD ROLL WEIGHED 2,000 POUNDS (907 KG). STRIPS WERE CUT 108 FEET (33 M) LONG, 42 INCHES (107 CM) WIDE, AND 1.5 INCHES (4 CM) THICK.

But it takes more than sightlines to give fans an optimal experience: Cleveland's new stadium boasted 948 toilets, 391 urinals, 204 sinks, 72 showers, and 51 drinking fountains.

Beyond Bathrooms

While the Tennessee Titans were one of the first teams to acknowledge that as many women as men may attend games — maybe more. As the team's new stadium was readied, the statistics were revealed. Of the 66 restrooms within the facility, 40 were for women.

Tennessee also acknowledged that the game experience extends beyond the stadium walls. When the Titans opened their new facility, the Adelphia Coliseum, for the start of the 1999 season, the team stressed the outdoor experience of their stadium. Publicity emphasized that the Coliseum was on the east bank of the Cumberland River across from downtown Nashville, and noted that more than 2,000 trees would be planted within the 105-acre (4.3-hectare) complex. The team even publicized the brand of natural grass selected for use on the field — no Astroturf for the Titans!

In the 1990s many NFL teams evaluated the details of their stadiums. Even facilities as new as the 1982-built Metrodome in Minnesota were declared outdated by new Vikings owner Red McCombs. He insisted that no remodeling job could make the stadium suitable for his team. This was one game that

ADDING TO THE THEME-PARK MOTIF AT TAMPA BAY'S RAYMOND JAMES STADIUM, EIGHT CANNONS ON ITS REPLICA PIRATE SHIP BOOM SMOKE, CONFETTI, AND FOAM FOOTBALLS INTO THE STANDS.

NFL opponents may have wanted McCombs to win, as teams agreed that Metrodome noise was among the loudest in the NFL.

Such stadium flaws often lead owners to demand new arenas. Jacksonville got its way in 1994. The Jaguars got the go-ahead to tear down the Gator Bowl, a college stadium built in 1920, and build in its place Alltel Stadium.

Old or new, stadiums are full of surprises. After building a new home in 1997, the Washington Redskins started making changes just two years later. Metal pipes found to obstruct sight lines were replaced with glass. The sound system was fine-tuned, and more JumboTron screens were added for the scoreboard section.

Pirates Invade Stadium

The Tampa Bay Buccaneers planned on surprises in their new Florida stadium. One year after opening in 1998, they launched plans to make their stadium offer much more than just football.

A year or so later, the Bucs unveiled a $3 million, 103-foot (31-m)-long pirate ship and Buccaneer Cove in the north end of the stadium end zone. A 20,000-square-foot (1,858-sq-m) area dressed up in beach huts offered food and souvenirs. The Buccaneers made their football stadium into a theme park, like other Florida amusement facilities.

Tampa Bay vice president Brian Glazer said to reporters, "We'd like a win at every game . . . but the key is to make the game experience the best you can make it. Baseball has done a lot of this in the past. They've tried to make the game experience better. We feel our game doesn't need that. But we want to do it anyway."

Glazer added, "We wanted our stadium to be unique and offer our fans tremendous game enhancements they would not find at any other sporting event. This ship will be the most recognizable stadium feature in the world. We believe it will become a symbol for the team, a source of pride for our players and fans — and an intimidation factor for visiting teams."

What will the newest sports palaces look like in the gridiron world? At the start of this century, the Cincinnati Bengals, Detroit Lions, Pittsburgh Steelers, San Francisco 49ers, and Seattle Seahawks were first in line with stadiums to be completed. Franchises know they can't promise a winning team, but they can promise a winning stadium.

4

PASSING THE BUCKS

Stadiums don't get built for free. Or do they?

Cities like having sports teams. City governments believe that teams create jobs and bring in out-of-towners who will spend money in the city. That's why local governments listen when a team says, "We need a new stadium. Build one — or we're going someplace else." Such threats often send elected leaders scrambling for ways to come up with the millions of dollars needed for new stadiums.

Taxes are the most common way in which governments raise money. City residents may get a chance to approve new taxes with a vote. That's why out-of-towners are often taxed first. Visitors who stay in hotels can't vote against a city's high hotel tax.

But even out-of-towners can find a way to have a say.

In 1997, Governor Gary Locke of Washington State wanted to help finance a new home for the Seattle Seahawks with a 10 percent tax on sports memorabilia and licensed sports clothing. The Nike sportswear company in the neighboring state of Oregon objected. The tax would make Nike products cost more for Seahawk followers — and many of those football fans came from Oregon. Worse, that kind of tax could set a dangerous example. What if other cities did the same, raising Nike prices for fans all around the country? The company and other business leaders complained loudly enough to kill the idea.

Whose Opinion Counts?

Voters don't always get an election to choose whether taxes should be used for new stadiums. Polls and surveys may be used to see if citizens want a new stadium. But these are sometimes paid for by the teams wanting the stadiums and may not truly represent the voters' wishes.

Sometimes stadium supporters get support by promising economic benefits they can't really guarantee. They might say, "NFL games in Cityville, USA, create $20 million in spending each season." But such figures may not mean new spending. If a family spends $200 at an NFL game, they may spend that much less at the mall or amusement park.

There are plenty of citizens who object when their tax dollars are being spent on sports. In the summer of 1999, Senator Arlen Specter, a Pennsylvania Republican, tried to find a way to make teams pay for at least half of their own stadiums. Specter spoke to the Senate Judiciary Committee, a group that studies how laws do and don't work. He revealed that football owners were collecting $17.6 billion for TV broadcast rights, spread over eight years. Specter prepared a bill that would force teams to use 10 percent of this jackpot to help pay for at least 50 percent of new stadium costs. State and city governments would pay up to 25 percent.

Senator Russell Feingold of Wisconsin objected to Specter's plan, claiming that his state's Green Bay Packers were a "small-market" team. The TV revenue was a bigger part of the Pack's total budget than it was for bigger teams. Giving up some TV profits might threaten the team's survival, he said.

"LUNCH BOXES, NO LUXURY BOXES"

"NFL OWNERS PLAY WITH YOUR OWN MONEY"

—PROTEST SIGNS WAVED IN LOS ANGELES IN 1999 OPPOSING THE NFL GETTING A PUBLICLY FUNDED NEW STADIUM BEFORE ADDING AN EXPANSION TEAM IN CALIFORNIA.

NFL commissioner Paul Tagliabue added in testimony before the Senate Committee that the league and its teams had provided more than $1.5 billion in the 1990s toward stadium construction and renovation.

Making team owners pay their own way in stadium-building is an idea that more government leaders are considering. In 1999 baseball's Minnesota Twins and the NFL's Vikings both wanted a new stadium to replace the 17-year-old Minneapolis Metrodome they shared. Minnesota governor Jesse Ventura said, "When I see a new Roosevelt High School, which is seventy-seven years old, then we'll talk about it." Ventura had attended the school, also in Minneapolis.

Paving the Way

Some teams do pay for new stadiums themselves. Redskins owner Jack Kent Cooke covered the entire $180 million cost for the team's new stadium. Nevertheless, the Redskins still benefited from millions of tax dollars.

FUNDS FOR BUILDING THE REDSKINS' STADIUM CAME FROM TEAM COFFERS. TAXES PAID FOR PARKING FACILITIES AND OTHER IMPROVEMENTS.

The state of Maryland added $70 million to the stadium's value by making new and bigger roads in and out of the facility, parking lots, and other transportation bonuses. Massachusetts offered a similar $70 million worth of road improvements to convince the New England Patriots to stay and build their own stadium.

Teams want citizens on their side. In fact, many teams employ lobbyists, people not directly associated with the team, to approach city, state, and federal governments for money. Lobbyists persuade mayors or governors that a new stadium should be built with public money. Then the government officials ask the public for stadium approval.

COOKE DIED BEFORE HE COULD SEE THE REDSKINS' NEW STADIUM OPEN IN 1997, WHICH IS WHY THE ARENA WAS FIRST NAMED IN HIS HONOR. THE 200 ACRES (81 HECTARES) WHERE THE STADIUM COMPLEX IS LOCATED WAS TO BE NAMED RALJON, A SEPARATE COMMUNITY. COOKE'S INTENT WAS TO HONOR HIS SONS, RALPH AND JOHN. BUT WHEN THE TEAM AND STADIUM WERE SOLD FOR $800 MILLION IN JULY 1999, CHANGE CAME FAST. THE NEW OWNER, DANIEL SNYDER, A THIRTY-FOUR-YEAR-OLD MARKETING EXECUTIVE, UNDERSTOOD THE POWER AND VALUE OF NAMES.

ONE MONTH AFTER HIS PURCHASE, SNYDER ANNOUNCED THAT HIS OWNERSHIP GROUP WOULD RENAME THE TEAM HOME REDSKINS STADIUM UNTIL NAMING RIGHTS COULD BE SOLD. NEXT, THE NAME RALJON WAS DROPPED BY THE TEAM. "RALJON WAS INTENDED TO BE A SHRINE TO HIS [COOKE'S] KIDS AND NOT FOOTBALL," SNYDER SAID. "THE CITIZENS . . . THAT LIVE THERE THINK IT'S INSULTING." IN A $200 MILLION DEAL FOR THE NAMING RIGHTS, THE STADIUM IS NOW CALLED FEDEX FIELD.

As time went by, team owners and government leaders began to wonder if education might beat the hard-sell game plan in getting the public to fund new stadiums. In 1999 the Vikings included "Stadium Chalk Talk" on their Internet Web site. The presentation fielded typical questions, such as, "The Vikings had a great season last year. Why do [you] need a new stadium?" The team offered easy answers to some complicated questions. It also encouraged on-line fans to subscribe for updated briefings on why a new stadium should be built.

Sometimes it seems that all a team has to do is ask for a stadium, and a city will give up some of its existing budget for the team.

The Oakland City Council agreed to spend $340,000 in 1961 to relocate Exposition Field, home of the Raiders. According to an Oakland newspaper, Raiders owners Ed McGah, Bob Osborne, and Wayne Valley had given the city a Thanksgiving Day deadline to decide if the Raiders would "play in Oakland in 1962 — or quit." The team would stay only if it got a better place to play. The owners hinted that the city of San Jose was ready to create a separate stadium and encourage the team to move there. By the week before Thanksgiving, an Oakland "citizens' study committee" approved using land once filled by a public housing project for Frank Youell Field. The City Council approved the plan, too.

No New Taxes?

Nevertheless, saying that the money used for stadium-building is "already there" can be confusing. Team spokes-people sometimes tell government leaders that new stadiums can be built with existing tax dollars with a plan called tax incremental financing (TIF). The public is happy, thinking they won't have to pay more taxes. What TIF really does, however, is to reassign how money will be spent. Money that supports schools or other government programs may be "redirected" to stadium construction.

Some cities have found stadium money without TIF or new taxes. In Baltimore, both the Ravens' PSINet Stadium at Camden Yards and baseball's Orioles Park were paid for, in large part, by gamblers. Proceeds from a sports lottery helped fund part of the stadium's estimated $220 million cost. The team's Web site carried ads for the lottery tickets, urging fans to "Scratch for the Ravens."

Cities will pay to gain old teams or new ones, and the NFL knows it. But each side has bargaining power. In 1999 the NFL offered Los Angeles an expansion team if the city would help build the new club a stadium. Los Angeles offered $150 million for parking and other improvements for the Memorial Coliseum in exchange for yearly rent of $2.5 to $5 million. The league balked, and the city's negotiator walked.

Meanwhile, Houston businessman Bud McNair was ready for the Los Angeles venture to fail. He convinced Houston's leaders to pony up $195 million toward a $310 million new stadium with a retractable roof, which is now under construction next to the Astrodome. Called the Harris County Stadium, it will seat 69,500 and is expected to open for the start of the 2002 season. The Astrodome had hosted the Houston Oilers until 1995, when Houston's mayor vowed not to subsidize a new stadium and the team moved to Nashville. Some Houston citizens wanted pro football back.

The prospective Houston team owner told reporters that if the expansion franchise finally did choose Los Angeles, an old NFL team would do just as well. "We'd immediately start talking to other teams," McNair said. "All you have to do is look at the facts. There are some teams with unsatisfactory stadium arrangements."

In the NFL, action matches team against team. In the stadium-building game, it's city versus city.

5

RUNNING WITH THE PACK

Teams start making game plans for new homes years ahead of schedule. Millions of dollars are at risk. Land must be purchased. Local and state governments must cooperate with zoning, transportation, and more. If one piece of the puzzle is missing, the entire project may fall through. That's why teams often don't reveal relocation plans until they must.

But the Green Bay Packers had to play the game of stadium planning by another set of rules. That's because the Wisconsin team is owned by its fans. Sort of.

The team first sold shares of stock to the public in 1949 as a way of raising money for operating expenses. By 1999 more than 111,000 people owned a total of 4.7 million shares of the Green Bay Packers Incorporated.

Stockholders don't get to vote on how the company is run. A seven-member executive committee and a 45-member board of directors oversee all team business. But because the Packers are a "publicly held" business, they are required to hold yearly stockholder meetings.

On July 7, 1999, 7,064 stockholders and guests gathered at Lambeau Field — a logical place for such a huge group of Packers fans to meet. Instead of posting statistics and game results on the JumboTron scoreboards, the audience looked to the screens for charts and figures outlining the team's financial standing. The main topic of discussion: Should historic Lambeau Field be renovated or be torn down to make room for a bigger, more modern facility?

To some, the question was ridiculous. Stockholders or not, fans love Lambeau Field. Every game there since 1960 has been a sellout.

The Cost of Change

Money was the primary concern: Would renovation cost more than rebuilding? The debate had been going on for months.

Before the 1998–1999 season, the Packers had announced major remodeling plans for Lambeau Field. The remodeling plans called for a new concourse, press box, stadium club restaurant, and additional stadium seating. Packers' President Bob Harlan had said, "It may take us as long as four or five years to complete what

ON JULY 7, 1999, THE GREEN BAY PACKERS INC. HELD A STOCKHOLDERS MEETING AT LAMBEAU FIELD TO DISCUSS WHETHER TO RENOVATE OR REPLACE THE STADIUM.

we want to accomplish, but the primary objective is to make the concourse a much larger and safer area for our fans. We expect that portion of the project to be completed for the season of 2000."

The concourse is important because all 61,000 fans use this as a common area when visiting Lambeau Field. The planned renovations would have increased the number of women's restrooms, doubled the number of concession stands, and created at least two retail stores. Harlan said he hoped the planned changes would keep Lambeau a profitable, practical home for another twenty to twenty-five years.

Plans on paper are always easier than plans in action, however. As architects began drawing up actual designs, they wondered where more luxury suites could fit into the snug stadium. And the same old question came back: Could a newer stadium, with more luxury suites, be built for less money than it cost to fix up the old? It was becoming clear to Packers management that no plan would be cheap. In February 1999, the team reported that renovations were on hold — and ticket prices were going up.

President Harlan knew that many, if not most, Packers backers wanted to save Lambeau Field. He knew the fans wouldn't stand for a domed stadium. Sure, Wisconsin may have been the iciest NFL venue ever. But fans liked it that way. It intimidated other teams.

The Stadium Race

At the shareholders meeting in July, President Harlan talked about money, pointing out that more seats might not be the answer. After all, NFL visiting teams get 40 percent of ticket sales. Even if the Packers' 60 percent share grew, it still might take years to earn back the cost of expanding the stadium. Harlan introduced the idea of offering perks like restaurants and luxury boxes to bring in more money to spend on player bonuses. And players are what a team is all about.

HOW DO YOU KNOW IF YOU'RE GETTING CLOSE TO LAMBEAU FIELD IN GREEN BAY, WISCONSIN?

THE CITY NAMED STREETS AFTER FORMER PACKERS.

Others suggested that Lambeau might be able to make money in a way that no new stadium ever could. The site had attracted more than 30,000 visitors in 1999, all before a single game had been played. The ninety-minute tour of Lambeau Field was a huge attraction in Green Bay.

But old stadium or new, more money was needed. Harlan announced that the team was likely to charge a personal seat license (PSL) on season ticket holders to raise more funds, as other NFL teams have done.

What is a personal seat license? Before being allowed to buy a season ticket, fans would be required to buy a PSL, which would entitle them to purchase the same seat location for a set number of years. Simply put: In order to keep their beloved season tickets, season ticket holders would have to make an additional "contribution" to the building or remodeling of a stadium. PSL prices charged by other teams ranged in the thousands of dollars.

As 1999 began, Green Bay believed that it could wait eight to twelve years before financial needs forced the building of a new or renovated stadium. But a month before the meeting with stockholders, the team told the local newspaper it saw ten years as Lambeau's maximum life span. At the meeting, stockholders were assured of only one thing: Green Bay would never have a domed facility. Subsequent plans were developed to renovate the stadium.

LUXURY SUITES, LUXURY BOXES. CALL THEM WHAT YOU WILL. NEITHER IS CHEAP. THE AVERAGE SUITE WILL SEAT TEN TO TWENTY-FIVE FANS. UPHOLSTERED CHAIRS, SLIDING-GLASS WINDOWS, BUFFET TABLES, SINK, REFRIGERATOR, ICEMAKER, COAT CLOSET, AND PRIVATE RESTROOMS ARE STANDARD FARE FOR SUCH CLASSY QUARTERS. SOME LUXURY SUITES HAVE WAITERS, COOKS, AND BARTENDERS. WARM, DRY FANS NEVER HAVE TO WAIT IN LINE FOR ANYTHING DURING A GAME IN THESE PRICEY AREAS.

OTHER TEAMS HAVE USED THE PSL WITH GREAT SUCCESS. JERRY "THE RAZOR" RICHARDSON PLAYED FOR THE BALTIMORE COLTS IN 1959 AND 1960. HIS SUCCESS AS CO-OWNER OF A SINGLE HAMBURGER STAND IN SOUTH CAROLINA BECAME THE BEGINNINGS OF THE NATIONAL FOOD FRANCHISE HARDEES. RICHARDSON BECAME OWNER OF THE CAROLINA PANTHERS EXPANSION TEAM IN 1993. THE TEAM MOVED INTO BRAND-NEW ERICSSON STADIUM IN 1996, ITS SECOND SEASON. THE STADIUM IS PRIVATELY OWNED, FINANCED BY THE SALE OF APPROXIMATELY $150 MILLION IN PERSONAL SEAT LICENSES.

DAMON "GREEK" TASSOS, GUARD-LINEBACKER FOR THE GREEN BAY PACKERS FROM 1947 TO 1949, TOLD ABOUT THE EARLY DAYS OF FOOTBALL IN WISCONSIN. IT WAS ALMOST A DIFFERENT WORLD:

"GREEN BAY'S CITY STADIUM WAS MADE OF LUMBER, 20,000 SEATS AND NATURAL GRASS. I SHOT SEVEN PHEASANTS ON THE 40-YARD LINE ONE DAY BEFORE PRACTICE," TASSOS SAID.

"GOALPOSTS WERE ON THE ZERO YARD LINE. WHEN THE FIELD 'FROOZE' [A WISCONSIN SLANG] THE FREEZE-LINE DEPTH WAS 3 FEET [0.9 M]. IT WAS LIKE PLAYING ON CONCRETE! [WE PLAYED] ALL-DAY GAMES.

"ALL THE OTHER FIELDS IN THE LEAGUE HAD GRASS. THE FREEZE LINE WAS THE SAME AND THE MAJORITY OF FIELDS WERE [ALSO] BASEBALL STADIUMS."

TASSOS'S FINAL SEASON WITH THE PACKERS WAS THE YEAR THAT CHANGED THE TEAM FOR DECADES AFTER. "IN 1949, THE PACKERS WERE BROKE AND COULD NOT PAY THE PLAYERS WITH FOUR GAMES LEFT ON THE SCHEDULE," TASSOS SAID. "COACH-OWNER 'CURLY' LAMBEAU FIRED SEVENTEEN PLAYERS OUT OF THIRTY-FIVE, SO THAT WE COULD GO BACK TO GREEN BAY. THAT SUMMER HE WENT TO THE PEOPLE FOR HELP — AND HE GOT HELP. HE INCORPORATED, AND SHARES WERE $1 EACH. THE PACKERS BECAME THE GREEN BAY PACKERS INCORPORATED. HE THEN PAID ALL DEBTS AND PLAYERS AND BECAME SOLVENT. THOSE WERE SPOOKY DAYS WITH NO TELEVISION [PROFITS]!"

6

SURPRISING STADIUMS

Math can be tricky. For example, if there are thirty-two NFL teams, that means there are only thirty-two places to see pro football action, right? Wrong!

The NFL is not the only pro football league in North America. The Canadian Football League (CFL) is an eight-team league with a long history. The history of pro football in Canada can be traced back to 1907, long before the NFL. In 1936 another league began just for teams in western Canada. The two leagues combined in 1958, making the CFL. The earliest Canadian pro football featured former rugby teams playing on cricket fields. The game of cricket is often described as a European relative to baseball. And just as NFL teams used reconfigured baseball fields, early CFL teams often adapted cricket fields.

The Ottawa Rough Riders were for years the Canadian pro team with the oldest stadium, Landsdowne Park, which opened in 1898 as part of a fairgrounds complex. Later, the name became Frank Clair Stadium, after a famed CFL coach of the 1960s. The stadium outlived the team. The Rough Riders went out of business in 1996. After Ottawa's demise, the Saskatchewan Roughriders held the reins of Canada's "oldest stadium" in Regina, where Taylor Field had been built in 1928.

Back in the United States, NFL players often make their first yearly appearances on fields belonging to the "Cheese League." This nickname applies to four teams that train at different colleges in Wisconsin, a state famous for dairy products. These preseason training camps begin in July.

The home-state Green Bay Packers first held training at St. Norbert College in DePere in 1958. Teams often train in their home states to get the feel of their home climates. But Wisconsin offers cooler summer temperatures than many other locales. Three out-of-state teams decided to beat the heat by going north to Wisconsin, making for unique preseason training camps where fans can find their heroes. The Bears have been at the University of Wisconsin-Platteville since 1984. The New Orleans Saints adopted a Wisconsin college training site in 1988, the Kansas City Chiefs in 1991.

One Game Only

Where else might pro football teams clash?

Two NFL teams return to football's birthplace each year for an exhibition. Canton, Ohio, is where the NFL was organized in 1920. The city now hosts the Pro Football Hall of Fame and Museum. Each August, on the same

THE CHICAGO BEARS BEAT THE HEAT BY TRAINING
AT THE UNIVERSITY OF WISCONSIN-PLATTEVILLE.

weekend when new members are inducted, Canton's Fawcett Stadium hosts a preseason exhibition game. The annual event began in 1962.

The postseason celebration for the league is the annual All-Star Game in Honolulu, Hawaii. Since 1980 the multipurpose Aloha Stadium has hosted this meeting of top players from the NFL's two divisions, the American and National Football Conferences.

NFL teams may even move their games to surprising sites for regular-season matchups. Stanford Stadium, used for college football, hosted one of the San Francisco 49ers' home games versus the New England Patriots in 1989. Days earlier, Candlestick Park had been damaged by an earthquake. Teams have also played on temporary fields while new stadiums were being built, giving more fans a chance to see professional ball.

Sometimes, a team's misfortune turns into a fan's lucky day.

7

WHERE WORK IS PLAY

"Linemen usually had their noses down, or into someone, so they didn't see much."

— Duane Putnam, Los Angeles Rams offensive
  guard 1952–1959, 1962; Dallas 1960; Cleveland 1961.

Not all players were too preoccupied with "work" to enjoy their unique worksites. Some players almost viewed their stadiums as second homes.

George Samuel Hughes played right guard and right tackle for the Pittsburgh Steelers from 1950 to 1954. According to this two-time All-Pro selection, "You could close your eyes and almost identify the different stadiums." He reserved special memories of Forbes Field, Pittsburgh's home stadium, which also housed the baseball Pirates.

"The loudest stadium, with very expressive fans!" Hughes recalled. "Forbes was old, cold, always snowy on the grassy field. Babe Ruth's monument was in the end zone. It helped make you try to play your best game."

From 1950 to 1959, Detroit's Lou Creekmur starred as a tackle and guard on offense and defense. Creekmur, a 1996 Hall of Famer, helped the Lions to three NFL titles.

Special Rooms

Because stadiums are like second homes, there are "rooms" most fans don't see. Chicago's Soldier Field, opened in 1924, hides an underground parking garage for players within the stadium.

After the final regular-season game in 1979, when the Bears defeated the Cardinals at home by a 36-point margin, the team showered and met in the garage. They crowded around a couple of their cars and tuned the radios to the Cowboys-Redskins game. The tension was heavy because if Dallas beat Washington, the Bears would go to the playoffs in a wild-card berth. That's how, in the cold, dark belly of the stadium, players turned into fans, holding their breath, cheering, hoping Dallas would win. It did, and so did the Bears.

Soldier Field, like many early urban stadiums, was squeezed into the heart of a city. There was little room in these old arenas for parking lot "tailgate" parties or the usual pregame celebrations that make current stadiums seem like amusement parks. In fact, some old stadiums were almost scary. Former Detroit Lion Lou Creekmur remembered: "The area around Tiger Stadium was not the best section of town. There was no really good parking area. Cars were in the streets and lawns."

From Baseball to Football

Neighborhood aside, Creekmur remembers that Detroit's stadium — designed for baseball — was a good fit for football. "Tiger Stadium converted well. [The field running] north to south gave the fans good seats. We had many crowds over 50- or 60,000," Creekmur said.

Not all baseball stadiums made such a smooth transition to football.

"The turf in some stadiums was really bad. . . . You would tear up 3-foot [0.9-m] sections of sod as you ran," Creekmur said. "That meant later in the year you played on

FOR OUTDOOR STADIUMS, THERE IS NO PERFECT LOCATION. FANS RAVE ABOUT THE VIEW OF LAKE MICHIGAN AT CHICAGO'S SOLDIER FIELD, BUT THE WATER INVITED DISASTER IN 1988. THE NFC PLAYOFF GAME, THE BEARS VERSUS THE PHILADELPHIA EAGLES, BECAME KNOWN AS "THE FOG BOWL." FEW FANS COULD EVEN SEE THE FIELD AS THE BEARS BEAT THE VISITORS, 20–12.

ONLY SINCE 1967 HAS THE NFL USED THE "SLINGSHOT" GOALPOST, WITH ONE CENTER UPRIGHT (INSTEAD OF TWO, MAKING A LETTER H) EXTENDING TO THE CROSSBAR. FORMER NFL COACH JIM TRIMBLE INVENTED THE SAFER GOALPOST.

the dirt. Many defensive linemen had a tendency to throw dirt in your face." Small wonder Creekmur believed that "the best fields were those where only football was played, like Los Angeles or Green Bay."

Offensive end Don Stonesifer pointed out that converted baseball stadiums often made for cramped quarters. Stonesifer played for the Chicago [now Arizona] Cardinals from 1951 to 1956 in old Comiskey Park. Before being torn down to become the parking lot for "new" Comiskey Park in 1990, Old Comiskey was best known for hosting baseball's White Sox. However, NFL games were squeezed into the converted stadium sporadically from 1922 through 1958. Stonesifer remembered how football games did — and didn't — fare on the field.

"If the baseball team was still involved in the playoffs, the baseball dirt paths were still on the field," he said. Just as bad, if not worse, "there was hardly any space between the end zone and the cement stands," Stonesifer said. "In Wrigley Field, you could not catch a pass deep in the end zone for fear of running into the stands."

But Stonesifer found a way to use obstacles to his advantage. Throughout the 1950s, goalposts were H-shaped and unpadded — and situated right on the goal line. "I would use the goalpost a lot when we were down on the opposing team's goal line, within ten yards or so," Stonesifer said. "By running a pass pattern and attempting to have the defender back into or run into the goalpost, I would be clear!"

Seeing the Light

Not all old stadium woes could be blamed on baseball.

Glenn Presnall logged six NFL seasons (1931–1936) playing offense and defense in some of football's first stadiums. "My memory of the lighting system at

Ironton [Ohio], where I started my pro career, was [that it was] very primitive," he said. "There were just flood-lights on the roof of the stadium. However, we just practiced at night and played games on Sunday [afternoons]."

Day games had their problems, too. Presnall served three seasons at Portsmouth, Ohio, before the team was transplanted, becoming the Detroit Lions. Portsmouth's Universal Stadium "was a frame building," Presnall said. "At one end of the field late in the season when it would snow, it would sift through the [building's] cracks and get on the bench. That made for a lot of discomfort."

Players in Cleveland's Municipal Stadium had similar woes. Municipal Stadium became known as the "Mistake on the Lake" because the cold winds off nearby Lake Erie haunted players on the field and off. Passing games shriveled while teammates shivered on the sidelines.

How did players keep warm on the sidelines?

Mike Phipps quarterbacked the Cleveland Browns from 1970 to 1976 and the Chicago Bears from 1977 to 1981. "Giants Stadium was the first place I encountered a heated bench," Phipps said. ". . . It felt like sitting on an electric blanket. . . ."

Phipps appreciated football both as a player and as a fan. "Believe me, the cold is worse for fans than players," he said. "I've seen enough games from the stands. You can't move. You're locked in your seats. Players can at least move around to get warm."

However, when the players can't get warm they get sneaky.

The 1934 NFL Championship Game, played at the horseshoe-shaped Polo Grounds, became known as "The Sneakers Game." In addition to a tough Chicago Bears lineup, the New York Giants were facing a frozen field, with a temperature of 9°F (-13°C) and wind gusts of 20 miles (32 km) per hour. How could they beat Chicago if they couldn't beat the elements? Blowing on his fingers, one player told how his college football team wore basketball shoes for on-field traction on wintry days.

By halftime, a Giants fan who worked in a nearby college athletic department had delivered 19 pairs of sneakers. Nine Giants found shoes that fit. The solid footing rallied the home team to beat the elements, and the Bears, 30–13.

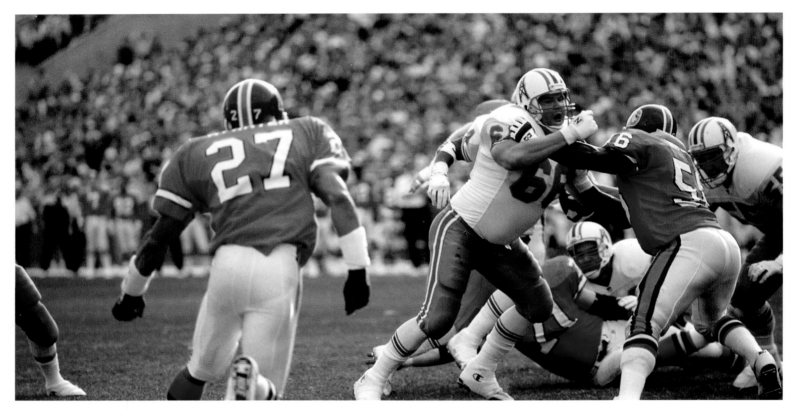

HOUSTON OILERS' OFFENSIVE GUARD DOUG DAWSON PLAYED ON ALL FIELDS: REAL AND
ARTIFICIAL TURF, FOOTBALL-ONLY, AND MULTIPURPOSE.

Learning Football's Ins and Outs

With the St. Louis Cardinals from 1984 to 1986, offensive guard Doug Dawson played outdoors on artificial turf. With the Houston Oilers in 1986 and from 1990 to 1993, his games were Astrodome affairs, indoors and on Astroturf. His last season, with the Cleveland Browns in 1994, was outdoors on real grass.

"I was a young kid, in junior high, when I played on Astroturf for the first time," Dawson remembered. "It was exciting. But the longer you play, the more you lean toward playing on grass. Grass is easier on your body as you get older. Astroturf grabs your cleats more. More ankle injuries happen. Another problem with artificial turf is the seams," created when the field is covered by huge rolls of artificial turf.

Having played on every type of field in the league, Dawson knew what he liked. "A place that was built just for football — somewhere like Tampa, with drainage and proper field aeration for its grass — that's an incredible surface to play on!"

"Seeing players with muddy uniforms and green stains, you know that's how football should be played — on natural grass," Dawson said.

Getting His Kicks in K.C.

Mike Eischeid, punter-kicker for the Oakland Raiders from 1966 to 1971 and the Minnesota Vikings from 1972 to 1974, knew that the battlefield can help determine the outcome of the war.

"I liked Municipal Stadium in Kansas City, where we played before they built Arrowhead," Eischeid said. "Fans were close. [That closeness] allowed you to get a better perspective of the field and the corners, for out-of-bounds punts. It wasn't like that in a spacious stadium like Soldier Field in Chicago. And the grass at Municipal Stadium was unbelievably groomed. Groundskeeper George Toma manicured it perfectly."

A well-groomed field helps players concentrate on the game, not on potholes or mudholes that could trip them up.

"In Minnesota, the groundskeeper was always a big part of things," Eischeid said. "He was around all the time. [Vikings head coach] Bud [Grant] always consulted with him. Because we practiced in Metropolitan Stadium, too, we kept the field covered with a tarp as much as possible."

STANDARD TOOLS IN ANY STADIUM ARE THE FIRST-DOWN "STICKS" AND CHAINS, USED TO MEASURE IF THE TEAM ADVANCED A FULL 10 YARDS. IN A 1972 PRESEASON GAME, BALTIMORE DEFENSIVE END BUBBA SMITH SUFFERED A YEAR-ENDING KNEE INJURY. HE TRIPPED ON THE TIGHTLY DRAWN CHAINS. THE NFL LATER RULED THAT THE STAKES SHOULD HAVE FLEXIBLE, RUBBER ENDS, AND NOW THE STAKES AND CHAINS ARE MORE BENDABLE AND SAFE.

Fields changed during Eischeid's career. "The Astrodome was the first-ever indoor stadium," he said. "Footing was always good [because bad weather was no longer a problem]. They called it Astroturf, but it was really indoor-outdoor carpeting. Today, artificial turf is refined, more like grass."

The stadiums built during Eischeid's career changed, too.

"When they built the Coliseum in Oakland, they made large locker rooms," he said. But in older places like Boston's Fenway Park, "those locker rooms should've housed ten people," he said, "not a team of forty-two and a coaching staff of eight. There was no room to walk! The facilities weren't built with football in mind.

"I've seen it all. Before Super Bowl VIII (1974), we practiced in a gymnasium that week. My locker there was a nail on the wall."

8

MORE THAN A GAME

Redskins fan Jim Siker spoke for fans of many sports when he said, "Attending a game in person should be more than just seeing a game." This is why he didn't like the new Jack Kent Cooke Stadium.

Jack Kent Cooke Stadium was built to keep fans in the section for which they bought a ticket. "To change sections, one must leave the field of play, go under the seats [through a hallway-like concourse], and emerge in the next section," Siker explained.

Perhaps designers wanted to keep fans who bought lower-priced tickets from moving into empty, expensive seats during the game. Perhaps designers wanted fans to walk by the food stands and souvenir sellers as often as possible, increasing the team's possible profits.

But what happened as a result of the design had some unintentional effects. A longtime tradition of pep parades around the entire stadium stopped.

"The 'U Crew' were garbed in team colors with a fake long arm topped with an oversized hand in the 'We're Number 1' position," Siker remembered. "There were three or four of them parading around at the end of the fourth quarter shouting 'You, You, You!,' pointing at fans and encouraging enthusiasm."

After moving to the new stadium, Redskins fans not only missed the U Crew but also Santas on parade and marching Hogettes. With no section-to-section access, all the parades that fans had grown to love came to an end.

"An enormously appealing facet of attending a live game is lost forever," Siker said.

The Eagles' Nest

Fans want more than "just seeing a game." Philadelphia Eagles fan Tom Collins is proof. In 1960, Collins saw his first pro football game at Franklin Field. He was one of 67,325 fans seeing the NFL Championship Game — the equivalent of today's Super Bowl — where Philadelphia beat visiting Green Bay, 17–13. It was more than just a game to the ten-year-old Collins.

Afterward, Collins got to visit the Eagles' locker room, getting a football signed by his favorite team. "The Eagles' locker room wasn't anything fancy," Collins remembered. "There were wooden benches for the players to sit and change their clothes on, old metal lockers, and a long shower stall with maybe a half dozen shower heads on both sides."

Outside the locker room, it wasn't much fancier.

"Franklin Field had hard wooden bleachers and in the wintertime a swirling wind swept the field," Collins said. But what went on at the field made up for the simplicity of the stadium. "Eagles games were very glitzy for the times. There were halftime activities that included high school bands and drill teams," Collins said. It didn't really matter that "the public address (PA) system was a step above two cans and a string. It was very hard to understand over the crowd noise" or that "the scoreboard, as I remember, was not as high-tech as the ones they use today.

"It got the job done," Collins said.

Redskins Park in Washington, D.C., later renamed Robert F. Kennedy Stadium, hosted its first Redskins game in 1961. In an article, "36,767 See First Game in Stadium," local reporter Jack Walsh called the new facility "magnificent." Yet he described a failed Redskins pass as one that "would have accomplished a second minor miracle at this stadium site." The first? "The first was getting it built."

THE ULTRAMODERN NEW YORK GIANTS STADIUM BUILT IN EAST RUTHERFORD, NJ, IN 1976 IS COMPLETELY ENCLOSED AND CAN SEAT MORE THAN 78,000 FANS. ALTHOUGH ITS ORIGINAL TURF WAS ARTIFICIAL, THIS HAS BEEN REPLACED WITH NATURAL GRASS.

Fields of Study

Football fans often become students of the game, studying plays and game plans, every detail of their pastime. The more that Lawrence Lee Jr. of Staten Island, New York, studied the game, the more he noticed differences in the places where football was played.

"For decades," he said, "pro football's teams played in the ballparks of their baseball counterparts." For example, football's Giants first played in the Polo Grounds, also home to baseball's New York Giants. "Very rarely did teams have stadiums of their own, and then only if the stadium had already been built for another purpose, such as the Los Angeles Coliseum. Football teams did not begin getting their own stadiums until the late 1960s to the early '70s.

"But by then," Lee said, "stadium-building ceased to have its own identity. So-called 'cookie-cutter' stadiums were now the norm."

For example, Lee said, the new Giants Stadium, "like most stadiums that are built for pro football only, really has no distinguishing characteristics of its own. It looks like so many other stadiums around the country. . . ."

Oddly, Lee said, having an unshared stadium may be a drawback.

"In the early part of football season, while baseball season was still on, you could see the dirt infield still there, usually on one end of the football field. It was fun to see how the stadium was set up differently for football and baseball," Lee said. "Patches of grass and dirt would be missing in different areas, in different stadiums. The best thing about a natural grass field is that no two looked alike."

Football Versus Baseball

Looking for differences draws fans in, asks them to draw conclusions and form opinions. Why do so many football stadiums look alike?

"One reason may be the playing field itself," Lee said. "In baseball, at least in theory, the foul lines extend indefinitely. The outfield measurements are determined arbitrarily. Combine this with the fact that [since] baseball parks originally had to be built within the confines of a city block, ballparks took on some very strange and individual shapes. But by the time football stadiums were built, structures like these were built on the outskirts of a city, near highway access, where there was no limitation to the design. And unlike baseball, football has a strictly defined playing field. So, basically a football field is laid out, and stands are built up, completely surrounding the field."

Giants Stadium, Lee said, "is completely enclosed. You can see nothing of your surroundings, except for the sky — if you look straight up. Even though you are outside, you feel 'closed-in. . . .'"

9

CAN FUTURE STADIUMS PRESERVE THE PAST?

"No!"

—The entire response given by the 1999 Chiefs office, when asked if there was a Hall of Fame in or around Arrowhead Stadium, or any exhibits, plaques, or statues honoring past players or Kansas City's football history.

Most fans will never get to chat with their team's star quarterback, or talk about game plans with the coach. But every year, thousands of fans have personal contact with a team's home — its stadium.

Fans might scan an arena's huge outsides while driving past, or even attend a game and sit inside. Millions more can study a stadium's features during TV broadcasts. Of course, people are the focus of most TV or radio broadcasts or newspaper or magazine stories. The stadium is only the background for interviews with coaches and star players. But players and coaches will disappear with injuries, retirement, or moves to a new franchise. Stadiums remain.

Stadiums are a part of football history. That fact is slowly sinking in with teams and institutions.

AN EXCAVATOR BREAKS GROUND IN 1999 FOR THE STEELERS' NEW FOOTBALL STADIUM NEXT TO THE SITE OF THE OLD STADIUM.

"At the Pro Football Hall of Fame, we have no exhibits dedicated to stadiums, and only a few stadium artifacts," Museum Collections Manager Jason Aikens said in 1999. "Our most prominent stadium artifacts are stadium seats from the old Cleveland Browns Stadium."

A Groundbreaking Groundbreaking

As the century turned, however, some teams were trying to make smoother transitions when changing from old stadiums to new, honoring the past instead of trying to bury it. On June 18, 1999, the Pittsburgh Steelers held public groundbreaking ceremonies for their new stadium, which was to spring up in part of the parking lot west of the old Three Rivers Stadium. Fans were invited to have their photos taken near the construction site while turning a shovelful of dirt. Even though the team would remain in its old stadium for two more seasons, the Steelers saw a chance to link the present with the future.

The Washington Redskins named each level of seats in their new stadium after a

BUCKY, THE WHITE FIBERGLASS BRONCO, ONCE STOOD MAJESTICALLY ATOP DENVER'S OLD MILE HIGH STADIUM SCOREBOARD.

former player or coach. The team also included a Hall of Fame museum within the building, and even dedicated the press box to Shirley Povich, a man who spent decades reporting on the team for various papers.

In Denver, the Broncos' planned replacement for Mile High Stadium also included a museum, where the team could display retired jerseys and other Broncos relics. One of the team's top pieces of memorabilia was Bucky, the white fiberglass horse that bucked on top of the scoreboard of their former stadium. He debuted in 1976 and was modeled after Trigger, the famous equine costar of movie-star cowboy Roy Rogers.

But sports museums have encountered some challenges in creating displays to preserve stadium history. Most vintage photos were shot from vantage points inside the stadium, to show part of the game action, not to highlight stadium architecture. Photographers of the past didn't always pay attention to a stadium's exterior, either.

Exterior stadium photos were often taken from the air. Aerial photography was growing in popularity at the same time that football was, in the first half of the twentieth century. Pictures from the sky show how a stadium fits into the surrounding cityscape, and also explain why stadiums are often called "bowls." The pictures seem to show a bowl with thousands of people balanced on its sides and a football field at the bottom.

Postcards from the past offer some of the best examples of football stadium photography, both from the sky and from a fan's-eye view: from a seat or approaching the front gate.

Sneaking Peeks at History

Chris Nichol started collecting stadium postcards in 1985. Fourteen years later, he had views of more than 3,500 college and pro stadiums in his collection. Nichol guessed that "70 to 75 percent" of his football stadium postcards were views from the sky.

"My favorite football card is an aerial of Kansas City's Municipal Stadium, shot during a Chiefs game in the late 1960s," he said. "There is a small insert of a players' huddle in the lower left-hand corner. Since this park was also home of baseball's Athletics from 1955 to 1966, this card is very sought-after by most baseball

Kansas City Chiefs at Municipal Stadium

Photo: Warner Studio

THIS HIGHLY SOUGHT-AFTER STADIUM POSTCARD FEATURES AN AERIAL VIEW
OF KANSAS CITY'S MUNICIPAL STADIUM, WITH AN INSERT OF A PLAYERS'
HUDDLE IN THE LOWER LEFT-HAND CORNER.

collectors. Its value is in the range of $20. There are bleachers set up in left field — a practice long since abandoned in today's modern parks. KC Municipal was seldom photographed, and this is simply a fantastic close-up view."

Nichol noted that successful teams don't always have easy-to-find stadium postcards. For example, Wisconsin's Lambeau Field, which opened in 1956, has had "a reasonable number of cards produced, but they are a bit tougher to come by. [That's because] Green Bay is a smaller town, and not as many visitors have passed through over the years," Nichol said.

"I am particularly interested in Lambeau cards because [the field] has had so many different expansions over the years, and postcards show a great history of each of the changes," he went on. "My collection of Lambeau cards [about twenty-five] probably shows six or seven different phases of expansion."

A famous team or stadium often makes for an assortment of easily available past images. "In terms of older stadiums, Soldier Field cards are relatively easy to come by across all eras," Nichol said. "Chicago being a prime tourist stop and transportation hub over the years, and the fact that the stadium is so centrally located and often photographed on the lakefront, are probably a couple of the reasons for the wide availability. Some of the tougher ones to come by are from the 1970s after the Bears moved in, when they set up temporary bleachers across one end zone before the facility was renovated with a permanent closed end and sky boxes."

GIANTS STADIUM MAY HAVE THE MOST FAMOUS, OR INFAMOUS, END ZONE OF ALL. UNION LEADER JIMMY HOFFA DISAPPEARED IN THE 1970S. MURDER WAS SUSPECTED. BECAUSE HOFFA DIED AS THE NEW JERSEY SITE WAS BEING BUILT, THE WILD BELIEF CONTINUED FOR DECADES THAT HIS BODY MIGHT BE BURIED UNDER ONE OF THE FIELDS.

THE 49ERS PLAYED IN CANDLESTICK PARK BEFORE IT WAS RENAMED 3COM. THE NAME STEMS FROM THE CANDLESTICK BIRD, WHICH ONCE WADED IN THE COVES AROUND SAN FRANCISCO BAY. ITS LONG, THIN LEGS AND CHICKEN-SIZE BODY MADE IT A HUNTER'S TREAT. BY THE 1950S, THE SPECIES HAD BEEN KILLED OFF.

THE CHARGERS CALLED THEIR HOME JACK MURPHY STADIUM FOR NEARLY THIRTY YEARS. MURPHY WAS A LOCAL SPORTSWRITER WHO CAMPAIGNED TO GET NFL FOOTBALL IN SAN DIEGO AND LATER CONVINCED THE CITY TO BUILD A NEW STADIUM.

While fans and activists often fail to convince cities and teams to save old stadiums, collectors have succeeded in saving parts of them. Imagine sitting in a seat from the former home of the Browns or the Broncos, years after the structure was torn down.

Grounds "Keepers"

Other hobbyists keep smaller reminders of stadium greatness. Some save chunks of artificial turf, with thoughts that great footballs and famed feet may have bounced upon the bits of green in years past. Several teams supplied their souvenir shops with tiny squares of the pretend grass that became too worn for game use. The teams knew that their trash could be a treasure for fans.

"Packers Paydirt" may top the list of strange stadium souvenirs. More than 11,000 jars of dirt from Lambeau Field were sold in 1999 for $9.95 each. The company marketing the soil souvenir shipped the product to all fifty states. However, because the U.S. government ruled that "Paydirt" was an agricultural product, the jars could not be shipped to foreign countries.

Some of the buyers said they wanted to sprinkle real Lambeau Field dirt on the graves of deceased Packers fans.

Fans want to feel close to their favorite team, as if a part of that team belongs to them. But fans also want mementos, physical objects that preserve memories, because even stadiums can vanish from sight.

At the University of Detroit a parking lot is lit by towers. Those towers once served Titan Stadium. The 1928 Detroit Wolverines and the Lions, from 1934 to 1937, depended on the college stadium as their NFL home.

It is a too-quiet tribute to a site that hosted football history. But, like Titan Stadium, most former stadium sites aren't commemorated in any way. No plaque, nothing. Until teams and cities begin to honor the palaces of sport, it will be up to the fans.

Today's fans can preserve the history of today's stadiums.

Tomorrow may be too late.

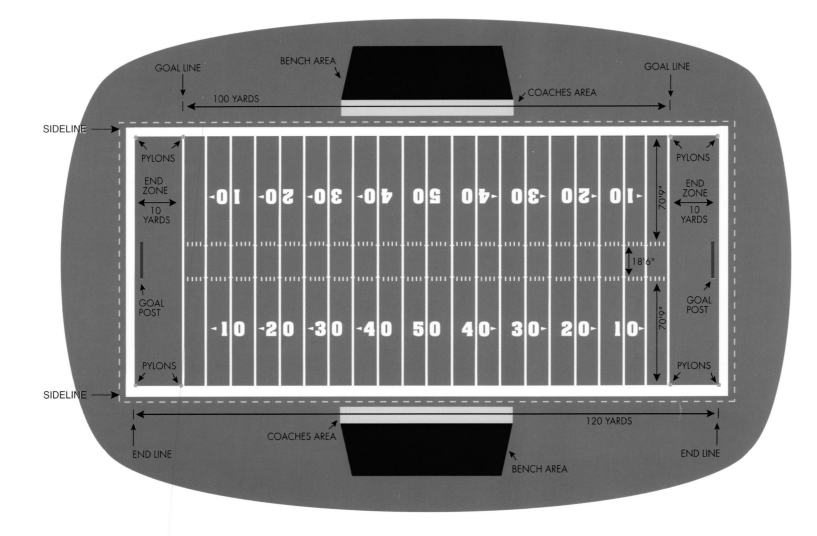

GOAL LINE
BENCH AREA
GOAL LINE
100 YARDS
COACHES AREA
SIDELINE
PYLONS
PYLONS
END ZONE
10 YARDS
END ZONE
10 YARDS
70'9"
18'6"
GOAL POST
GOAL POST
70'9"
PYLONS
PYLONS
SIDELINE
COACHES AREA
120 YARDS
END LINE
BENCH AREA
END LINE

DIAGRAM OF A PROFESSIONAL FOOTBALL FIELD

According to official National Football League rules, a playing field must be 360 feet (110 meters) in length and 160 feet (49 meters) in width. Field markings, including 5 and 10 yard lines, hashmarks, sidelines, and the solid border around the field, must be clear and distinct. Bench areas must be provided for both the home and visiting teams. Goal posts stand on the end lines behind the goal lines.

For Further Information

Books

Cagan, Joanna and Neil deMause. *Field of Schemes*. Monroe, ME: Common Courage Press, 1998.

Carroll, Bob, Michael Gershman, David Neft, and John Thorn, editors. *Total Football: The Official Encyclopedia of the National Football League (First Edition)*. New York: HarperCollins, 1997.

Lowry, Phillip J. *Green Gridirons*. North Huntington, PA: Professional Football Researchers Association, 1990.

Morgan, Jon. *Glory for Sale: Fans, Dollars and the New NFL*. Baltimore: Bancroft Press, 1997.

Whittingham, Richard. *The Bears: A 75-Year Celebration*. Dallas: Taylor Publishing, 1994.

Internet Resources

www.ballparks.com
This Web site offers an excellent introduction to all stadiums (past, present, and future), including lots of photos and reprinted newspaper articles about stadium happenings.

www.fieldofschemes.com
Authors of the book with the same title host this Web site. Current news about teams wanting governments to pay for their stadium building is included. However, it's no mystery how this Web site feels about who should pay for new stadiums!

www.footballresearch.com
Web site of Pro Football Researchers Association. PFRA publishes newsletters and books. The membership studies different subjects from pro football history, including stadiums.

www.hok.com
To learn more the stadium creations and renovations of this famous architectural firm, start with the company's official Web site.

www.nfl.com
The official National Football League site includes links to individual team sites.

Index

Page numbers in *italics* refer to illustrations.

Adelphia Coliseum, Nashville, Tennessee, 6, 17, *18–19*, 19
Aerial photography, 55
Aikens, Jason, 54
All-Star Game, Honolulu, Hawaii, 36
Alltel Stadium, Jacksonville, Florida, 20
Aloha Stadium, Honolulu, Hawaii, 36
American Football Conference, 36
Americans with Disability Act (ADA), 8
Arrowhead Stadium, Kansas City, 43, 52
Artificial turf, 8, 36, 42–43, 58
Astrodome, Houston, Texas, 27, 42, 44
Astroturf, 42–44

Baltimore Colts, 32
Baltimore Ravens, 9, 26
Browns Stadium, Cleveland, Ohio, 6, 10–11, *11*, 16–17
Bucky (fiberglass horse), *54*, 55
Buffalo Bills, 5

CAD (computer-aided design), 15
Canadian Football League (CFL), 33
Candlestick Park, San Francisco, California, 36, 58

Carolina Panthers, 32
"Cheese League," 34
Chicago Bears, *35*, 35, 39, 41, 57
Chicago (now Arizona) Cardinals, 40
Cincinnati Bengals, 21
City Stadium, Green Bay, Wisconsin, 32
Cleveland Browns, 16, 41, 42
Cleveland Municipal Stadium, 16, 17, 41
Collins, Tom, 47
Comiskey Park, Chicago, Illinois, 40
Cooke, Jack Kent, 24, 25
Creekmur, Lou, *38*, 39–40

Dallas Cowboys, 7, 39
Dawson, Doug, 42, *42–43*
Denver Broncos, 55
Detroit Lions, 21, *38*, 41, 59
Detroit Wolverines, 59

Eischeid, Mike, 43–44
Ericsson Stadium, Charlotte, North Carolina, 6, 32
Exposition Field, Oakland, California, 26

Fawcett Stadium, Canton, Ohio, 36
FedEx Field, Washington, D.C., 6, 24, *24–25*, 25, 45–46, 54–55
Feingold, Russell, 23
Fenway Park, Boston, Massachusetts, 44
Forbes Field, Pittsburgh, Pennsylvania, 37
Frank Clair Stadium, Ottawa, Canada, 33
Franklin Field, Philadelphia, Pennsylvania, 36, 47
Frank Youell Field, Oakland, California, 26
Friederich, Peter, 12–15

Gator Bowl, Jacksonville, Florida, 20, 34
Giants Stadium, East Rutherford, New Jersey, 4, 41, *48–49*, 50, 57
Glazer, Brian, 21
Goalposts, 40, 50
Golden Gate Park, San Francisco, California, 7
Grant, Bud, 43
Grass, 4, 8, 17, 19, 42–43, 50
Green Bay Packers, 23, 28–30, 32, 35, 47, 58
Groundskeeper, 8, 43

Harlan, Bob, 29–31
Harris County Stadium, Houston, Texas, 27
Hoffa, Jimmy, 57

HOK Sports Facilities Group, 6–15

Houston Oilers, 27, 42

Hughes, George Samuel, 37

Jack Kent Cooke Stadium (*see* FedEx Field, Washington, D.C.)

Jack Murphy Stadium, San Diego, California, 58

Jacksonville Jaguars, 20

Joe Robbie (Pro Player) Stadium, Miami, Florida, 11

Kansas City Chiefs, 6, 35, 52, 55, *56*

Kansas City Municipal Stadium, 43, 55, *56, 57*

Kezar Park, San Francisco, California, 7, 8

Labinski, Ron, 9

Lambeau, 'Curly', 32

Lambeau Field, Green Bay, Wisconsin, 28–31, 57, 58

Landsdowne Park, Ottawa, Canada, 33, *34*

LED (light emitting diode) screens, 7, 9

Lee, Lawrence, Jr., 4–5, 50–51

Locke, Gary, 22

Luxury suites, 31

Martins, Alex, 16

McCombs, Red, 19–20

McGah, Ed, 26

McNair, Bud, 27

Memorial Coliseum, Los Angeles, California, 27, 50

Mile High Stadium, Denver, Colorado, *54,* 55

Minneapolis Metrodome, 19–20, 24

Minnesota Twins, 24

Minnesota Vikings, 19–20, 24, 26, 43

Models, 12–15

Namath, Joe, *4*

National Football Conference, 36

New England Patriots, 25, 36

New Orleans Saints, 35

New York Giants, 41, 50

New York Jets, 4, *4, 5*

Nichol, Chris, 55, 57

Nike sportswear company, 22–23

Oakland Raiders, 26, 43

Oriole Park, Camden Yards, Maryland, 8–10, 26

Osborne, Bob, 26

Ottawa Rough Riders, 33

Pep parades, 45–46, *46*

Personal seat license (PSL), 31, 32

Philadelphia Eagles, 36, 47

Phipps, Mike, 41

Pittsburgh Pirates, 37

Pittsburgh Steelers, 21, 37, 54

Policy, Carmen, 17

Polo Grounds, 41, 50

Postcards, 55, *56, 57*

Povich, Shirley, 55

Preseason training camps, 35

Presnall, Glenn, 40–41

Pro Football Hall of Fame and Museum, Canton, Ohio, 35

PSINet Stadium, Baltimore, Maryland, 6, 8–10, 15, 26

Putnam, Duane, 37

Raymond James Stadium, Tampa Bay, Florida, 6, *13, 20,* 21

RCA Dome, Indianapolis, Indiana, 36

Redskins Park, Washington, D.C., 47

Richardson, Jerry "The Razor," 32

Robert F. Kennedy Stadium, Washington, D.C., 47

Ruth, Babe, 37

St. Louis Cardinals, 39, 42

San Diego Chargers, 58

San Francisco 49ers, 7, 8, 21, 36, 58

Saskatchewan Roughriders, 33

Scoreboards, 7–8, 20

Seattle Seahawks, 21, 22

Shea Stadium, Flushing Meadow,
    New York, 4, 4–5, 5

Siker, Jim, 45–46

Site selection, 6–7

Smith, Bubba, 43

Snyder, Daniel, 25

Soldier Field, Chicago, Illinois, 17, 39, 43, 57

Sound system, 20

Specter, Arlen, 23

Sports lottery, 26

Stanford Stadium, California, 36

Steelers Stadium, Pittsburgh, Pennsylvania,
    15, 53, 54

Stonesifer, Don, 40

Tagliabue, Paul, 24

Tampa Bay Buccaneers, 21

Tassos, Damon "Greek," 32

Taxes, 22–23, 26

Tax incremental financing (TIF), 26

Taylor Field, Canada, 33

Tennessee Titans, 19

Texas Stadium, Dallas, Texas, 7

Three Rivers Stadium, Pittsburgh,
    Pennsylvania, 54

Tiger Stadium, Detroit, Michigan, 39

Titan Stadium, Detroit, Michigan, 59

Toma, George, 43

Trimble, Jim, 40

TWA Dome, St. Louis, Missouri, 6, 8

Universal Stadium, Portsmouth, Ohio, 41

University of Detroit, 59

University of Pennsylvania, 36

University of Wisconsin-Platteville, 35, 35

Valley, Wayne, 26

Ventura, Jesse, 24

Walsh, Jack, 47

Washington Redskins, 20, 24, 39, 45–47,
    54–55

Wellner, Dennis, 6–8, 11

World Football League, 34

Wrigley Field, Chicago, Illinois, 40